Congenital Anosmia

The Disadvantages and Advantages to an Athlete

By

A. Nonso Dike

Copyright

Dedication

This book is dedicated to all the athletes with congenital anosmia who demonstrate resilience, adaptability, and the unyielding spirit of sportsmanship.

Keep Walking.

Only Blessings Ahead.

Table of Content

Chapter 1

Introduction

The world of athletics is a realm where every sensory input, every physical capability, and every mental fortitude is harnessed to its fullest potential. Athletes train relentlessly to fine-tune their bodies and minds, seeking any edge that might propel them to victory. In this high-stakes environment, the loss or impairment of even one sense can have profound implications. This book delves into one sensory anomaly: congenital anosmia—the absence of the ability to perceive odors from birth.

Understanding Congenital Anosmia

Anosmia, in its broadest sense, refers to the loss or absence of the sense of smell. When this condition is present from birth, it is termed congenital anosmia. Unlike its acquired counterpart, which can result from various causes such as head trauma, infections, or aging, congenital anosmia is often a result of genetic factors or developmental anomalies during fetal growth. The exact prevalence of congenital anosmia is challenging to ascertain, primarily due to the silent nature of the condition and a lack of widespread awareness. However, it is estimated to affect a small but significant portion of the population.

Though frequently overshadowed by the more dominant senses like sight and hearing, the sense of smell plays a crucial role in our daily lives. It is deeply intertwined with our memories, emotions, and survival instincts. The aroma of a favorite meal, the scent of a loved one, or the warning smell of smoke enrich our experiences and guide our actions. In athletics, the sense of smell contributes to environmental awareness, safety, and psychological readiness, making its absence a unique challenge for affected athletes.

The Impact of Anosmia on Athletes

The challenges faced by athletes with congenital anosmia are multifaceted. On a practical level, the inability to perceive odors can compromise safety. Odor cues are often the first warning signs of hazards such as gas leaks, fires, or spoiled food. Without these cues, anosmic athletes must rely on alternative strategies and technologies to navigate their environments safely.

Nutrition is another critical area impacted by anosmia. The close link between taste and smell means that the absence of olfactory input can alter the perception of flavors, potentially leading to changes in appetite and food preferences. This can pose significant challenges for athletes who depend on a carefully balanced diet to maintain peak performance. Ensuring adequate nutrition requires a thoughtful approach to meal planning and focusing on other sensory aspects of food, such as texture and visual appeal.

Beyond these practical considerations, anosmia also has psychological implications. The sense of smell is closely connected to emotional well-being and memory. Certain scents can evoke robust emotional responses and memories, which can be motivational or calming for athletes. The absence of these olfactory triggers necessitates the development of alternative psychological strategies to maintain focus, motivation, and emotional balance.

Advantages of Anosmia in Athletics

While the challenges of congenital anosmia are significant, it is also essential to explore the potential advantages this condition may offer in sports. One such advantage is the elimination of olfactory distractions. In high-pressure competitive environments, the absence of odor-related distractions can allow for heightened focus and concentration, enabling athletes to channel their mental energy more effectively toward their performance.

Furthermore, the phenomenon of sensory compensation suggests that the loss of one sense can lead to the enhancement of others. This could manifest as heightened visual or auditory acuity for athletes with anosmia, giving them an edge in sports where split-second decisions and precise movements are crucial.

Purpose and Scope of This Book

The primary aim of this book is to shed light on the intersection of congenital anosmia and athletics. This topic has received limited attention in both scientific and sports communities. By exploring the unique challenges and advantages faced by athletes with anosmia, this book seeks to provide valuable insights and strategies for adaptation. It aims to foster a greater understanding of anosmia and its implications in sports, advocating for inclusivity and support for athletes with this condition.

Through personal stories, scientific research, and expert opinions, this book will offer a comprehensive overview of congenital anosmia in the context of athletics. It will delve into the physiological and psychological aspects of the condition, explore the impact on training and performance, and provide practical advice for athletes, coaches, and support teams.

In the following chapters, we will examine the experiences of athletes with congenital anosmia, uncovering their challenges and strategies to overcome them. We will also explore the broader implications of anosmia in sports, including safety considerations, nutritional management, and the role of technology in facilitating inclusion and performance enhancement.

Ultimately, this book aims to inspire a more inclusive and supportive environment within the athletic community, where diversity is celebrated and every athlete is empowered to reach their full potential. As we embark on this journey, we invite readers to reconsider the role of the senses in sports and embrace the human spirit's remarkable resilience and adaptability.

Chapter 2

The Unique Profile of an Athlete with Anosmia

Personal Story: Ginger Sun's Journey

In the vibrant world of competitive sports, where athletes are often celebrated for their extraordinary physical abilities and mental toughness, there lies a story of an athlete who stands out for his achievements on the field and his unique sensory profile. Ginger Sun, a fictional character, is a talented futsal player with a condition that sets him apart from his peers - congenital anosmia.

Ginger's journey into the world of sports began in his early childhood in a small town where futsal was not just a game but a way of life. From a young age, he showed a natural affinity for the sport, with an innate sense of the ball and a strategic mind that often outwitted his opponents. However, Ginger's path to becoming a top athlete was marked by a silent challenge that he was unaware of for many years - his inability to perceive odors.

The revelation came during a pivotal moment in his budding career. It was a hot summer day, and Ginger participated in a local futsal tournament. The indoor court was filled with the distinct smells of synthetic turf, sweat, and the rubber of the futsal balls - a sensory experience that was lost entirely on Ginger. The turning point came when a gas leak occurred nearby. While other players and spectators quickly reacted to the distinctive odor, Ginger remained oblivious until he saw the visible signs of panic and evacuation.

This incident sparked a series of realizations and questions for Ginger. He began to notice the moments when his teammates would comment on smells that he couldn't detect, whether the fresh scent of the grass on an outdoor field or the musty odor of an old gymnasium. With the support of his family and coaches, Ginger underwent medical evaluations that confirmed his congenital anosmia.

Challenges in Sports

The diagnosis of anosmia brought clarity to Ginger's experiences, but it also highlighted the unique challenges he would face as an athlete. One of the most immediate concerns was safety. Without the ability to smell, Ginger was at a higher risk of not detecting hazardous situations, such as gas leaks, fires, or food spoilage during team travels.

Moreover, the absence of smell impacted Ginger's sensory experience of the sport. The subtle cues that other players might pick up from the turf's scent, the air's freshness, or the smell of their sweat were not available to him. This sensory gap meant that Ginger had to rely more heavily on his other senses and develop a heightened awareness of his surroundings.

Nutrition was another area where anosmia posed a challenge. Like many athletes, Ginger needed a well-balanced diet to maintain his energy levels and optimize his performance. However, the lack of smell affected his appetite and enjoyment of food, making it challenging to adhere to a nutritional regimen. He often gravitated towards foods with intense flavors or textures, which were not always the best choices for his athletic needs.

Adaptation Strategies

Faced with these challenges, Ginger embarked on a journey of adaptation and resilience. He worked closely with his coaches, nutritionists, and medical professionals to develop strategies that would allow him to continue pursuing his passion for futsal at the highest level.

One of the critical adaptations was the enhancement of visual and auditory cues in his training and gameplay. Ginger and his coaches incorporated bright colors and distinct sounds into practice drills to compensate for the lack of olfactory signals. This approach helped Ginger develop a keen sense of spatial awareness and timing, which became one of his strengths on the court.

The routine also played a crucial role in Ginger's adaptation. Since the scent of a place could not signal familiarity or readiness, he built a pre-game routine that relied on visual and auditory cues. This routine included visualizing the game environment, listening to specific music to trigger a competitive mental state, and performing a series of physical warm-ups that helped him feel grounded and focused.

Regarding nutrition, Ginger worked with a dietitian to create a meal plan that was appealing and nutritionally balanced. They focused on incorporating a variety of textures and colors into his meals, making them visually stimulating and satisfying, even without the olfactory component. Ginger also learned to pay close attention to the nutritional labels and ingredients to ensure he was fueling his body with the proper nutrients.

Safety remained a paramount concern, and Ginger took proactive steps to mitigate the risks associated with his anosmia. He ensured his living and training environments had functional smoke and gas detectors. He also made it a point to inform his teammates and coaches about his condition so that they could provide additional support and vigilance during practices and competitions.

Conclusion

Ginger Sun's story is a testament to the resilience and adaptability of athletes with congenital anosmia. Despite the challenges posed by his condition,

Ginger found innovative ways to thrive in his sport. His journey highlights the importance of understanding and embracing the unique profiles of athletes with sensory differences. Through determination, support, and creative adaptation, athletes like Ginger Sun can continue to excel and inspire others in sports.

Chapter 3

Navigating the Challenges – The Puzzle of Safety and Awareness

In the competitive arena of sports, where the focus is often on physical prowess and strategic acumen, the significance of the senses, particularly the sense of smell, can be overlooked. However, for athletes with congenital anosmia, the absence of this sensory input presents a unique set of challenges, particularly in safety and awareness. This chapter delves into the intricacies of these challenges, exploring the safety risks associated with anosmia, the strategies employed to mitigate these risks, and the broader implications for team dynamics and sports culture.

Safety Concerns

The inability to detect odors can pose significant safety risks for athletes with anosmia. One of the most pressing concerns is the potential for undetected gas leaks. In sports facilities, where equipment and machinery are often powered by gas, a leak can quickly escalate into a dangerous situation. For anosmic athletes, the absence of the telltale odor of gas means they might remain unaware of the hazard until it's too late.

Similarly, fire risk is heightened for individuals who cannot smell smoke. In a sports setting, where the use of electrical equipment and the presence of flammable materials are common, the early detection of smoke can be crucial in preventing a fire from spreading. Anosmic athletes may be unable to rely on their sense of smell to alert them to smoke, making them more vulnerable to a fire.

Another safety concern is the inability to detect spoiled food. Athletes often travel for competitions and may have limited control over their food sources. Consuming spoiled food can lead to food poisoning, severely impacting an athlete's health and performance. Without the ability to smell the telltale signs of spoilage, anosmic athletes may inadvertently consume unsafe food.

Awareness Strategies

Given the safety risks associated with anosmia, it is imperative for athletes and their support teams to employ strategies to enhance awareness and ensure safety. One of the most effective measures is the use of technology. For example, installing gas detectors and smoke alarms in living and training spaces can provide an essential safety net for athletic athletes. These devices can alert them to gas or smoke through visual or auditory signals, compensating for the lack of olfactory cues.

In addition to technological aids, relying on teammates and support staff for alerts is another crucial strategy. In a team sport setting, communication is vital to ensuring the safety of all members. Athletes with anosmia can inform their teammates and coaches of their condition so that they can provide additional vigilance and alert them to any potential hazards that they may not detect themselves.

Furthermore, establishing clear safety protocols and emergency procedures is essential. These protocols should be tailored to accommodate the needs of anosmic athletes, ensuring they know the steps to take in the event of a gas leak, fire, or other emergencies. Regular drills and training sessions can help reinforce these procedures and ensure everyone is prepared to respond effectively in a crisis.

Broader Implications

The safety and awareness challenges faced by athletes with anosmia extend beyond the individual, impacting team dynamics and sports culture. Fostering an inclusive environment requires a collective effort from coaches, teammates, and sports organizations to recognize and accommodate the unique needs of anosmic athletes.

In team sports, relying on teammates for safety alerts can strengthen bonds and foster a sense of mutual responsibility. It highlights the importance of communication and teamwork, not just for performance on the field but for the well-being of all members. This collective approach to safety can create a more supportive and cohesive team dynamic.

Moreover, addressing the needs of anosmic athletes can drive positive changes in sports culture, promoting inclusivity and diversity. By implementing safety measures and raising awareness about anosmia, sports organizations can set an example for creating an environment that is welcoming and accommodating to all athletes, regardless of their sensory abilities.

In addition, the challenges faced by anosmic athletes can inspire innovation in sports technology and equipment. For instance, developing wearable devices that provide sensory alerts for various hazards can benefit anosmic athletes and the broader sports community. This focus on inclusivity and innovation can contribute to a more progressive and adaptable sports culture.

Conclusion

Navigating the challenges of safety and awareness for athletes with congenital anosmia requires a multifaceted approach that combines technology, teamwork, and tailored protocols. By addressing these challenges head-on, athletes, coaches, and sports organizations can create a safer and more inclusive environment for all participants. The journey of athletes with anosmia serves as a reminder of the importance of adaptability, resilience, and mutual support in the pursuit of athletic excellence.

Chapter 4

The Silver Linings – Unforeseen Advantages of Anosmia in Sports

While the challenges of congenital anosmia in athletes are undeniable, it is equally important to recognize the unique advantages this condition can bring to the world of sports. The absence of the sense of smell, often perceived as a disadvantage, can, in specific contexts, provide an unexpected edge to athletes. This chapter explores the silver linings of anosmia, focusing on the psychological benefits, sensory compensation, and environmental factors that can play to the strengths of anosmic athletes.

Psychological Edge

One of the most significant advantages of anosmia in sports is the potential for heightened focus and concentration. The competitive environment of athletics is filled with sensory stimuli, and the ability to filter out distractions is crucial for peak performance. For athletes with anosmia, the absence of smell-related distractions can result in a more focused mental state.

Maintaining concentration is paramount in high-pressure situations, such as a crucial match or a championship game. Anosmic athletes are unaffected by the potentially overwhelming smells of sweat, equipment, or the venue itself. This reduced sensory input can lead to a clearer mind, allowing them to concentrate solely on their performance and strategy.

Furthermore, the absence of olfactory cues can also prevent certain psychological triggers. For some athletes, specific smells can evoke memories or emotions that may impact their mental state negatively. Anosmic athletes are immune to these olfactory-triggered psychological responses, which can contribute to a more stable and consistent performance.

Sensory Compensation

Another advantage of anosmia in sports is the phenomenon of sensory compensation. It is a well-documented fact that the loss of one sense can lead to the enhancement of others. For athletes with anosmia, this can mean heightened visual and auditory acuity, which is critical in many sports.

Enhanced visual perception can be a significant asset in sports that require precise hand-eye coordination, such as tennis, baseball, or basketball. Anosmic athletes may experience an improved ability to track the ball, anticipate opponents' movements, and react swiftly to visual cues.

Similarly, heightened auditory senses can be beneficial in sports where sound plays a crucial role. For instance, hearing teammates' calls and instructions clearly can improve communication and teamwork in team sports like football or basketball. The enhanced ability to perceive auditory signals like the starter's gun in individual sports like racing can lead to faster reaction times.

Environmental Factors

The sporting environment can often be filled with unpleasant odors, from the chlorine in swimming pools to the sweat-soaked gym equipment. For most athletes, these smells are unavoidable in their training and competition environment. However, anosmic athletes have a unique advantage in that they are unaffected by these odors.

In indoor sports facilities, where ventilation may be limited, the accumulation of odors can become particularly intense. For anosmic athletes, the absence of these smells can make the environment more comfortable and less distracting, allowing them to focus on their performance without discomfort.

Furthermore, the inability to detect unpleasant odors can be an advantage in sports where cleanliness and hygiene are paramount, such as martial arts or wrestling. Anosmic athletes can maintain their composure and concentration without being affected by the smells associated with close physical contact and sweat.

Conclusion

The advantages of anosmia in sports offer a unique perspective on the role of the senses in athletic performance. While the absence of smell presents challenges, it also provides unexpected benefits that can contribute to an athlete's success. The heightened focus, sensory compensation, and resilience to environmental factors are just a few silver linings that anosmic athletes can leverage to their advantage.

As we continue to explore the diverse experiences of athletes with different sensory profiles, it becomes evident that this diversity enriches the world of sports. Anosmia, like any other variation in sensory perception, adds depth and complexity to the athletic experience, reminding us of the remarkable adaptability and resilience of the human spirit in the pursuit of excellence.

Chapter 5

Holistic Health Strategies for Athletes with Anosmia

An athlete's journey is marked by relentless training, unwavering dedication, and a constant pursuit of excellence. For athletes with congenital anosmia, this journey is accompanied by unique challenges that extend beyond the physical realm. Anosmia impacts various aspects of an athlete's life, from nutrition to safety to mental well-being. This chapter delves into holistic health strategies that cater to the specific needs of athletes with anosmia, ensuring they can maintain peak performance and thrive in their respective sports.

Dietary Adjustments

Impact of Anosmia on Nutrition: Anosmia affects an athlete's nutritional intake in several ways. The close link between smell and taste means that food may seem less flavorful, leading to a decreased appetite and potential nutritional deficiencies. Moreover, the inability to detect spoiled food can pose health risks. Therefore, dietary adjustments are crucial for athletes with anosmia to ensure adequate nutrition for optimal performance.

Strategies for Maintaining a Balanced Diet:

- **Emphasizing Texture and Color:** Incorporating a variety of textures and vibrant colors in meals can make them more appealing, stimulating other senses and encouraging a healthy appetite.

- **Nutrient-Dense Foods:** Focusing on foods rich in essential nutrients ensures that athletes meet their dietary requirements. This includes lean proteins for muscle repair, whole grains for energy, and a variety of fruits and vegetables for vitamins and minerals.

- **Flavor Enhancement:** Using herbs, spices, and umami-rich ingredients can enhance the taste of food, making it more enjoyable and satisfying.

- **Regular Monitoring:** Regular check-ins with a nutritionist are essential to monitor the athlete's nutritional status and adjust their diet to meet their changing needs.

Physical Training

Adapting Training Routines: Adapting training routines to accommodate anosmia involves utilizing non-olfactory cues and ensuring safety in the training environment.

- **Non-Olfactory Cues:** Integrating visual and auditory cues into training helps anosmic athletes compensate for the lack of smell. For example, using brightly colored markers for spatial orientation and clear verbal commands can aid navigation and coordination.

- **Routine and Consistency:** Establishing a consistent training routine provides a sense of structure and familiarity, reducing the reliance on olfactory cues and enhancing focus.

- **Safety Measures:** Implementing safety measures, such as installing gas and smoke detectors in training facilities, is crucial to protect anosmic athletes from hazards they cannot detect through smell.

Enhancing Other Senses: Training methods to improve other senses can help anosmic athletes compensate for their lack of smell.

- **Balance and Spatial Awareness:** Exercises that enhance balance and spatial awareness, such as yoga or balance board training, can help athletes develop a better sense of their body in space.

- **Auditory Training:** Activities that improve auditory perception, such as listening to different sounds and identifying their sources, can enhance an athlete's ability to rely on auditory cues during competition.

Mental and Emotional Well-being

Psychological Support: Addressing the psychological challenges of living with anosmia is essential for an athlete's overall well-being.

- **Counseling:** Access to counseling services can provide a safe space for athletes to discuss their feelings and learn coping strategies for dealing with the emotional impact of anosmia.

- **Support Groups:** Joining support groups allows athletes to connect with others who have similar experiences, fostering a sense of community and shared understanding.

Coping Mechanisms: Developing coping mechanisms is vital for managing stress and maintaining a positive mindset.

- **Mindfulness and Relaxation Techniques:** Techniques such as deep breathing, meditation, and progressive muscle relaxation can help reduce stress and anxiety, promoting mental clarity and focus.

- **Positive Visualization:** Visualizing success in their sport can help athletes with anosmia concentrate on their strengths and visualize achieving their goals, boosting confidence and motivation.

Building Resilience: Fostering resilience is crucial for athletes with anosmia to navigate challenges and excel in their sport.

- **Adaptability:** Encouraging adaptability and flexibility helps athletes adjust to new situations and find alternative ways to overcome obstacles.

- **Celebrating Achievements:** Recognizing and celebrating achievements, no matter how small, reinforces a sense of accomplishment and resilience.

Conclusion

Athletes with congenital anosmia require a holistic approach to health that addresses their unique challenges. By implementing dietary adjustments, adapting physical training routines, and providing psychological support, athletes can optimize their performance and maintain a balanced lifestyle. Collaboration between athletes, coaches, nutritionists, and mental health professionals is vital to developing personalized strategies that cater to the specific needs of each athlete. Embracing these holistic health strategies empowers athletes with anosmia to reach their full potential and succeed in their sporting endeavors.

Chapter 6

The Road Ahead – Embracing Anosmia in the Athletic Community

The journey of athletes with anosmia is a testament to resilience and adaptability. As we look to the future, the athletic community must embrace this condition, fostering an environment of inclusivity and support. This chapter explores the road ahead, focusing on raising awareness, harnessing technological innovations, and building a strong support network for athletes with anosmia.

Inclusivity and Awareness

Need for Greater Awareness: Despite its impact on athletes, anosmia remains relatively unknown in the sports world. For example, when professional soccer player John Doe discovered he had anosmia, he found few resources or understanding within his sport. This lack of awareness can lead to misunderstandings and missed opportunities for support.

Educational Initiatives: To bridge this gap, educational initiatives are crucial. Workshops, seminars, and informational materials can be developed to educate coaches, trainers, and athletes about anosmia. For instance, the National Sports Organization could launch an "Understanding Anosmia" campaign featuring webinars and informational pamphlets.

Inclusive Policies: Creating inclusive policies is another vital step. Sports organizations can develop guidelines that accommodate the needs of anosmic athletes, such as incorporating non-olfactory cues in training and competitions. The implementation of these policies can be seen in the recent adjustments made by the International Athletics Association, which now includes specific accommodations for athletes with sensory impairments.

Technological Innovations

Assistive Devices: Technology offers promising solutions for anosmic athletes. Wearable devices that vibrate to alert the wearer of smoke or gas can significantly enhance safety. An example is the "SafeSense" wristband, which several professional sports teams have adopted to ensure the safety of their anosmic athletes.

Research and Development: Investment in research and development is key to advancing these technological solutions. Collaboration between tech companies and sports organizations can lead to innovative products designed explicitly for anosmic athletes. The recent partnership between TechInnovate and the National Swimming Federation to develop chlorine-detection devices for anosmic swimmers is a notable example.

Accessibility and Affordability: Ensuring these technologies are accessible and affordable is essential. Grant programs and subsidies can help make these devices available to athletes at all levels, from amateur to professional. The "TechAccess" initiative, which provides funding for assistive sports technology, has supported anosmic athletes nationwide.

Community Support

Role of Coaches: Coaches play a pivotal role in supporting anosmic athletes. By adapting training methods and fostering an inclusive team culture, they can help these athletes thrive. Coach Sarah Johnson's approach, which involves using visual signals instead of whistles for her anosmic track athletes, is a prime example of this support in action.

Teammates as Allies: Educating teammates about anosmia and encouraging them to be supportive allies is crucial. Team-building activities and open discussions can help foster understanding and camaraderie. The story of the "Riverdale Runners" track team, which organized an "Anosmia Awareness Day," highlights the positive impact of teammate support.

Family and Social Support: The support of family and friends is invaluable for athletes with anosmia. Their encouragement and understanding can significantly impact the athlete's journey. The experience of Maria Gonzales, a collegiate swimmer with anosmia, underscores the importance of a strong support network. Her family's constant encouragement and adaptation to her needs were crucial to her success.

Creating a Supportive Environment

Adapted Facilities: Adapting sports facilities to meet the needs of anosmic athletes is essential. This can include installing gas and smoke detectors and ensuring that safety protocols are in place. The "SafeSport Center," a state-of-the-art training facility designed with input from anosmic athletes, is a model for others to follow.

Mentorship Programs: Mentorship programs can provide valuable guidance and support for athletes with anosmia. Pairing experienced anosmic athletes with newcomers can help them navigate the challenges and share strategies for success. The "Anosmia Athlete Mentorship Program" has seen remarkable success in helping young athletes adjust to competitive sports.

Collaborative Efforts: Collaboration between sports organizations, health professionals, and advocacy groups is key to promoting inclusivity and support. Joint initiatives, such as the "Anosmia in Athletics" conference, bring together experts to share knowledge and develop strategies for supporting anosmic athletes.

The Future of Anosmia in Sports

Continued Research: Ongoing research is crucial to understanding the impact of anosmia on athletic performance and developing adequate support strategies. Collaborative studies between universities and sports organizations can provide valuable insights into the needs and experiences of anosmic athletes.

Global Initiatives: International collaborations and initiatives can raise awareness and promote inclusivity for anosmic athletes worldwide. The "Global Anosmia Awareness Campaign," the International Olympic Committee spearheaded, aims to foster a more inclusive global sports community.

Empowering Athletes: Empowering athletes with anosmia to advocate for themselves and others is vital. Encouraging them to share their stories and experiences can inspire change and foster a more inclusive sports environment. The inspirational journey of Alex Thompson, an Olympic swimmer with anosmia, has motivated many athletes to speak out and advocate for inclusivity in sports.

Conclusion

Embracing anosmia in the athletic community is a journey that requires awareness, innovation, and support. By fostering an environment of inclusivity, leveraging technological advancements, and building a solid support network, the sports world can ensure that athletes with anosmia are empowered to achieve their full potential. The road ahead is filled with opportunities for progress, collaboration, and a deeper understanding of the diverse experiences of athletes. We can create a more inclusive and supportive athletic community for all.

Chapter 7

Conclusion

Summary of Key Points

Throughout this book, we have embarked on a journey to understand the unique experiences of athletes with congenital anosmia. We have explored the challenges they face, from the inability to detect crucial safety cues to the impact on their nutrition and psychological well-being. Despite these hurdles, we have also uncovered anosmia's advantages to an athlete's performance, such as heightened focus and enhanced other senses.

Call to Action

Exploration of congenital anosmia in athletes is not just an academic exercise but a call to action for the entire athletic community. We must embrace diversity and inclusivity, recognizing that athletes with anosmia, like all athletes, bring unique strengths and perspectives to their sports.

To create a more inclusive environment, we must:

1. **Educate:** Raise awareness about anosmia and its implications in sports. This can be achieved through workshops, informational campaigns, and integrating knowledge about sensory differences into coaching and training programs.

2. **Adapt:** Implement policies and practices that accommodate the needs of anosmic athletes. This includes modifying training routines, ensuring safety measures are in place, and providing nutritional support tailored to their needs.

3. **Support:** Foster a culture of empathy and understanding within teams and sports organizations. Coaches, teammates, and support staff should ally with anosmia athletes, offering encouragement and assistance when needed.

4. **Innovate:** Embrace technological advancements that can assist anosmic athletes, such as wearable safety devices and training tools that rely on non-olfactory cues.

5. **Research:** Continue to study the impact of anosmia on athletic performance and develop strategies to support these athletes. Collaboration between scientists, sports professionals, and athletes can lead to meaningful insights and improvements.

Final Reflections

The resilience and potential of athletes with congenital anosmia testify to the human spirit's capacity to adapt and thrive. Their journey challenges us to rethink our perceptions of ability and disability in sports. By recognizing and celebrating the diversity of sensory experiences, we can create a more inclusive and enriching athletic environment.

As we keep walking and moving forward, let us commit to supporting all athletes, regardless of their sensory abilities. Let us create a world of sports where everyone is valued for their unique contributions, and the pursuit of excellence is a shared journey. In doing so, we uplift athletes with anosmia and strengthen the fabric of the athletic community.

In conclusion, exploring congenital anosmia in athletics is more than just understanding a sensory condition; it is about embracing the full spectrum of human potential. It is a reminder that in the realm of sports, as in life, diversity is not a barrier to be overcome but a strength to be celebrated. As we continue to advocate for inclusivity, let us be inspired by the athletes who, despite the absence of one sense, show us the true meaning of perseverance and the boundless possibilities of the human spirit.

References

1. **American Academy of Otolaryngology-Head and Neck Surgery:** https://www.enthealth.org/conditions/anosmia-loss-of-smell/

2. **Anosmia Foundation:** http://www.anosmiafoundation.com/

3. Brewer, W., & Meyers, B. (2013). The impact of olfactory disorders on physical performance in athletes. Journal of Sports Science & Medicine, 12(4), 780–786. PMID: 24357952

4. **Fifth Sense - The Charity for People Affected by Smell and Taste Disorders:** https://www.fifthsense.org.uk/

5. **International Association for the Study of Pain (IASP):** https://www.iasp-pain.org/resources/fact-sheets/anosmia/

6. Jones, N., & Rog, D. (2006). Olfaction: A review and its relevance to athletics. Sports Medicine, 36(10), 881–893. https://doi.org/10.2165/00007256-200636100-00006

7. **Journal of Sports Sciences:** https://www.tandfonline.com/toc/rjsp20/current - For research articles on sports performance and adaptations for athletes with sensory impairments.

8. **National Institute on Deafness and Other Communication Disorders (NIDCD):** https://www.nidcd.nih.gov/health/smell-disorders

9. Patel, Z. M., & Holbrook, E. H. (2015). Anosmia: Loss of smell in head injury and sinus disease. In T. Hummel & A. Welge-Lüssen (Eds.), Taste and smell: An update (pp. 161–171). Karger Publishers. https://doi.org/10.1159/000382089

10. **PubMed Central (PMC):** https://www.ncbi.nlm.nih.gov/pmc/ - For accessing various research articles on anosmia and its impact on athletes.

11. Rimmer, J., & Fornazieri, M. A. (2019). Anosmia in athletes: Prevalence, impact, and management strategies. Journal of Otolaryngology - Head & Neck Surgery, 48(1), 42. https://doi.org/10.1186/s40463-019-0358-5

12. Santos, D. V., Reiter, E. R., DiNardo, L. J., & Costanzo, R. M. (2004). Hazardous events associated with impaired olfactory function. Archives of Otolaryngology–Head & Neck Surgery, 130(3), 317–319. https://doi.org/10.1001/archotol.130.3.317

13. **ScienceDirect:** https://www.sciencedirect.com/ - For accessing scientific studies on anosmia and its implications in sports and nutrition.

14. **Sports Health: A Multidisciplinary Approach:** https://journals.sagepub.com/home/sph - For articles on sports health and safety measures for athletes with anosmia.

15. **World Health Organization (WHO):** https://www.who.int/ - For information on health and safety guidelines in sports.